Birdsongs

Birdsongs

Christine Tran

Birdsongs

© Christine Tran 2020

Published by
Lighthouse Christian Publishing
SAN 257-4330
5531 Dufferin Drive
Savage, Minnesota, 55378
United States of America

www.lighthousechristianpublishing.com

For:

Derek, my gift from above.

Alice, who inspired me to write.

Mother & Father, who always believe in me.

Matthew, who gives me laughter.

Lament

1. Lily
2. Sleepless
3. Blind
4. Heart
5. Fear
6. Pain
7. Constant
8. Sorrow
9. Leper
10. Luke 7:47
11. The Garden
12. Corona
13. Virus
14. Hope Deferred
15. Revive

Tribute

16. To Me
17. For Mother
18. For Father
19. For Brother
20. A Good Woman
21. A Good Man
22. For Derek

44.Gift
45.Unravel
46.Marry
47.Float
48.Water
49.Fire
50.Steadfast
51.Overcome
52.Rise
53.Freed
54.Tethered
55.It Is Well
56.Heal
57.Redeemed
58.Cling
59.Conduit
60.Scarlet
61.Forever Kingdom
62.Light
63.Illuminates
64.Conquered
65.Dream
66.Prophecy
67.Sages
68.Road
69.Cup

Lily

I cry out in distress,
As my thoughts sink and depress.
All around me is disorder,
Where is my Comforter?
He who watches the sparrow,
Also sees my sorrow.
He who tends to the lily,
Will care for me fully.

Sleepless

Sleepless is the night.
Gone is the morning light.
Deafening is the silence,
Rest is far in the distance.
Calm, heart; peace, be still,
And lift your eyes to the hill.
Lay down your weary head,
Find rest in Him instead.

Blind

I remember when I went blind,
It was a darkness of a terrible kind.
My own face I could not recognize,
The whole world was in disguise.
I slowly forgot the light,
And was losing the will to fight.
I felt I was hell-bound,
When darkness did surround.

Heart

The heart is but a vessel,
Science deems it a muscle.
Yet how deeply can it ache,
How fragmented it can break.
You can divide it piece by piece,
The grief never seems to cease.
On my heart, can you fix and operate?
Wake me from this comatose state.

Fear

Fear is a thief and a liar.

It drowns you in the muck and mire.

It says you are poor and weak;

Hopefulness you can never seek.

But perfect love casts out fear,

A love that clings close and near.

A love purchased by sinless blood,

A love that defeats fear with a flood.

Pain

There is a pain strong and fierce,
Through bone and marrow it does
pierce.
You lie in bed in languor,
Though tired, you are stirred to anger.
Helpless, you shake your fists at the
sky.
Either you or the pain must die.
Sitting in darkness, your soul awaits,
For the glimmering hope of heaven's
gates.

Constant

Pain is a constant friend,

Its companionship does not end.

Even when I want to separate,

It binds me to me through love and
hate.

Like a thief, it robs me of my sleep,

When I long for rest so deep.

I dream of a day when it will depart,

That pain will cease and my life can
start.

Sorrow

O, my soul, why do you mourn?

Why do you grieve with a heart

forlorn?

To see my Savior upon that cross,

Sorrow chokes as an overgrown moss.

He carried my pain and shame,

That I may call upon His Holy Name.

For me, He bled and died.

In Him, I shall dwell and abide.

Leper

I am the leper living in exile,
Life no longer felt worthwhile.
My wounds did fester and taint,
Alone, my heart grew faint.
Mockingly they called me unclean,
Everything changed when he arrived
on the scene.
With just a touch, I was fully healed.
Alive anew, I dance in the field.

Luke 7:47

Her many sins, He wholly forgave;
Her shame was buried in the grave.

She may have sinned like the harlot,
And her follies bled like scarlet.

In Him, she was made clean.
White as snow, new, and pristine.

Though she had transgressed,
His love and mercy was expressed.

The Garden

In the Garden, He wept tears of blood,
As anguish overflowed as a flood.
He was beaten and despised,
His love for us was all he surmised.
His body broken as He wore a crown
of thorn,
He died so that our hope may be borne.
He bore all our grief and sorrow,
That we may have an eternal
tomorrow.

Corona

All around is the stench of death,
The sick are too weak to take a breath.
The virus attacks and overtakes,
There is no room for mistakes.
The people are shaken aa they
succumb,
This pandemic, can we overcome?
Alone at home, we wrestle and cope.
For a brighter tomorrow, we dream
and hope.

Virus

A killer virus has overtaken the land,

Lives drifting away like grains of sand.

We are not granted entry at the gate,

And required to quarantine and isolate.

Left alone to our thoughts and fears,

Hope falls upon deaf ears.

All we hear are angels crying,

As our land bleeds with death and

dying.

Hope Deferred

The light is dimmed and hope is
deferred,
This was not the spring we preferred.
We were awaiting the flower's bloom,
Yet this illness has cast an impenetrable
gloom.
The brilliant minds are wrestling and
helpless,
As this virus destroys and brings
madness.
Where will our help come from?
Our hearts long for the eternal
kingdom.

Revive

This was not what we hoped for,
With dreams lying on the floor.
Visions and wild imaginations
Dancing on hills with thrilling
sensations.
Now we walk in the valley, low in the
pit,
We're more broken than we'd like to
admit.
Won't you come and revive us again?
Illuminate us like sunshine in the glen.

To Me

I will soon be some decades old,

That will be a day to behold.

I have tasted and seen that God is
good,

Though I may not follow as I should.

I have seen mercy and grace,

The kindness of His embrace.

Every day I am made new,

To rise and see the morning dew.

For Mother

Your love is relentless and strong,
You never lead me wrong.
Your words ring clear and loud,
Your love for me is unashamed and
proud.
You have taught me beauty and grace,
No matter the trials you face.
Your heritage will lead me
forevermore,
I will reap the hope you bore.

For Father

I am my father's daughter,
We are like two drops of water.
His thoughts run deep and wise,
His love is never in a disguise.
His affection is always made known,
He likens me to a queen on the throne.
For me, he would gladly die,
That life would never pass me by.

For Brother

We swiftly named you "Matthew,"
And you showed us colors of every
hue.
Who knew a little baby boy,
Could generate so much joy?
Your wit and wisdom run deep,
You will soar with a running leap.
There is no limit to what you'll do,
This sister will always remain true.

A Good Woman

A good woman is hard to find,
She knows her own mind.
She lives by truth and grace,
No matter what she may face.
She dances upon the hill.
She is the bird perched on your sill.
If you catch her burning glow,
Promise to never let her go.

A Good Man

A good man is truly rare,
One who shows his tender care.
He loves with a love so fierce,
Yet his words are soft and never pierce.
In courage and kindness, he leads,
He tends to your qualms and needs.
He will cling to you until your dying
day,
He will walk with you the everlasting
way.

For Derek

Our meeting was serendipitous;
Your words were kind and felicitous.
You came with a warm, fragrant smell.
I could love you, I could tell.
You stood tall like an oak tree.
With you, I could be uninhibited and
free.
I did not want to bid farewell;
The thought of you made my heart
swell.

For Alice

Today I will venture and embark
On a journey away from the dark.
I bid goodbye to the abyss,
And welcome in joy and bliss.
I choose to leave the pain behind,
And choose sight where I once was
blind.
I take a breath and step toward the
light
My lungs expand and my soul takes
flight.

For Baby Jo

Your soul, may He bless and keep.

In sweetness, may you sleep.

May you stay still and calm,

Surrender every doubt and qualm.

May you love what is gracious and
just,

He will bring you beauty from the
dust.

May you be courageous and brave,

For He has saved you from the grave.

For Lisa

Words cannot express my remorse,
"I am sorry" went and took its course.
I do not mean to cause you pain,
Now I wait for you in the rain.
All I see is your retreating back,
The sky we saw was bleeding black.
If I never see you again,
I wish you all the best, my old friend.

For Edward

They said you were a hero in the war,
But her heart you ripped apart and
tore.
Why did you have to leave,
On that fated summer's eve?
Because of you, she's orphaned and
fatherless,
Your love and tender touch she did
miss.
Today we visit you at the grave,
And pray that God your soul did save.

For April

Your friendship is fragrant and true,

You lift my spirits when I am blue.

In my burdens, you carry and bear,

Wisdom and insight do you share.

You see my muck and mire,

Yet never judge only admire.

I thank God for a friend like you,

You deserve all the blessings you are

due.

For Jean-Marie

For all the faith you had in me,
I can dream and fly freely.
For all the books you put on my shelf,
You believed in me, when I couldn't
myself.
In you, I found the beauty of words,
From the brilliant sky to the flight of
birds.
Thank you for inspiring thought,
Thank you for all the truth you taught.

Yellow

Today, the sky seems yellow.
The breeze is easy and mellow.
The birds are conducting a song,
I feel tempted to sing along.
Even as the pain is acute,
I will not be silenced and mute.
Even as the winds rage and roar,
My soul will ascend and soar.

Lemons

When life delivers lemons, you bake,

Ricotta cookies or a Bundt cake

Life is a little sour, a little sweet;

Let it out on the eggs you beat.

Be careful as you scoop and measure,

So that your bake can be a treasure.

To others, your treat is a delight;

Joy and pleasure in every bite.

Madeleine

With a madeleine in hand,
I drift to a distant land.
Dipped into a cup of milk and tea,
I enter into reverie.
I remember the distant past,
Memories that will surely last.
With the sound of dreams, my soul
awakes,
The ground quivers and reality breaks.

Tea

None could comfort like a cup of tea.

It always calms and eases me.

Jasmine, oolong or earl grey,

Tea over coffee any day.

It can quell and soothe,

With a taste silky and smooth.

With an aroma rosy and sweet,

I hope you and tea can one day meet.

Hazelnut

This morning, I had a cup of hazelnut
coffee.
The taste was fine and lofty.
A spoonful of sugar and some milk,
The taste was refined as silk.
With a slice of buttered toast,
My soul was warmed by this roast.
With this cup, my morning did bloom,
As sunshine streamed into the room.

Chocolate

The chocolate cake is so decadent,
One would think it's heaven sent.
Your innards are soft and sweet,
What a synapse when you and coffee
meet.
You are bitter enough to remind me of
life,
If only there were no pain and strife.
For now, in you I will enjoy,
I will savor the sweetness you employ.

Weeds

The weeds emerge every spring,
They're treated like an unwanted
thing.
They spread like fire and a disease,
Their pollen propagates through the
breeze.
Their will to live should be applauded,
Their relentlessness should be lauded.
Fight on and survive like the weeds,
Being steadfast is what your soul
needs.

Mustard Seed

May you be like the mustard seed,
Water and sunlight are all you need.
From a seedling into a tree,
May you grow up to be free.
May you bear much good fruit,
And establish a firm root.
You will stand steadfast until the last
day,
Even as the Earth gives way.

Leaf

May your sorrow and grief,

Dry up and shrivel like an autumn leaf.

Let there be water where it was once

dry,

Till the soil and the bird will pry.

May your harvest teem and abound;

At the feast table, your children will

surround.

Yesterday's hope seals tomorrow's

song,

The angels' choir you will prolong.

Sequoia

I admire the sequoia tree
That stands so tall and free.
His stature is so proud,
Yet he is never loud.
His heritage is quite old;
He's seen prophecies foretold.
He is quiet and lost in thought,
But he will forsake me not.

Harvest

May your harvest be abundant,

Joy expressed is never redundant.

Richly may your bounties flow,

May your skin soak in the sun's glow.

Let your pantry teem with daily bread,

Let your worries be put to bed.

May your soul lack no good things,

That you will swim in the hope

tomorrow brings.

Stars

At the million stars, I do marvel.

Though small, they are not bashful.

From galaxies distant and far away,

They shine bright like the sun of day.

They gleam from some cosmic shore,

The darkness craves for light once

more.

With the brilliance of the stars, I

dream,

No matter how hopeless it may seem.

Northern Lights

I long to see the Northern Lights,
My eyes can swim in the brilliant
sights.
I want to wade in the celestial shore,
Where every galaxy is an open door.
Where the stars are acquainted and call
me friend,
I fly in darkness and there is no cosmic
end.
The astral lights will lead me home,
My heart is still, there is only shalom.

Come What May

Come what may,
My love won't sway.
Come what may,
My heart will stay.
Come what may,
We'll face the day.
Come what may,
We'll find the way.

As Such

What love is this,
Stolen with a kiss?
That makes my heart soar,
And causes an uproar.
All within me is aflutter,
Words do fail and stutter.
Simply with just one touch.
Yes, love is as such.

Gift

There is such a love,
A perfect gift from above.
Every laugh and every smile
Makes your life worthwhile.
A kind of love that will endure;
A kind that is righteous and pure.
A kind of love I hope you find,
That your souls are ever intertwined.

Unravel

My tangled mess you do unravel,

For me, the distance you would travel.

If I ever feel down and blue,

You would bind to me so true.

If I get lost in my sea of thoughts,

You would wade and jump across.

If all my hopes suddenly deplete,

You would ensure my joy is complete.

Marry

You say to me, "Let's get married."
No sweeter words have been carried.
I imagine being your wife,
And facing the wind and strife.
Tomorrow cannot be planned,
But our dreams and fancies are not
grand.
We long for a life good and simple,
Where love abounds and runs ample.

Float

She floats with effervescence,
She graces you with her presence.
Her thoughts you cannot catch,
Her wits you cannot match.
She will never leave or forsake you,
Her covenant binds true.
She will take you by the hand,
Fly to great heights and never land.

Water

My sins float down the Jordan River,
And my flesh is cleaned with myrrh.
Parched, I take a drink.
I am more refreshed than I could think.
Life courses through my bloodstream,
My skin glows from the sun's beam.
I will never again thirst,
For he loves me at my worst.

Fire

I am walking barefooted through the
fire,
I sweat and my limbs, they tire.
Like gold, I am being made pure.
Thus, I must strive and endure.
I am being polished and refined,
Perfected by the Creator's mind.
I will leave behind the ashes and dust,
Press on, I will and must.

Steadfast

Press on and be steadfast,
Your strength will surely last.
Hold on and ever hope,
Keep climbing when you reach the
slope.
When all flee, you will remain;
Your perseverance will not wane.
As all slumber in forgetfulness,
You will keep watch in vigilance.

Overcome

This, we shall overcome;
To evil we will not succumb.
In all the chaos and noise,
We will not lose our poise.
Even as the war rages on,
Our courage will never be gone.
For goodness, we will wage the fight,
Darkness will not overtake the light.

Rise

As the storms retreat,

Again I rise from defeat.

Gone is impending doom,

As I see the orchards bloom.

Hope will once more arise,

As sorrow shrinks in demise.

My eyes look to the hill,

And my heart is beating still.

Freed

She used to lie and steal.

Fight hard for every meal.

She used to cheat and manipulate,

Schemes she would orchestrate.

Behold, when she saw the light.

Darkness and sin took flight.

The truth had set her free,

And healed her infinitely.

Tethered

Though the road is beaten and
weathered,
To Him my soul is tethered.
Though my soul is prone to tire,
Gold is refined through the fire.
He calls me His treasure,
And loves me beyond all measure,
While I writhe in pain,
He will strengthen and sustain.

It Is Well

Let us say, "it is well."

Love is stronger than hell.

Courage runs swift and deep,

Our souls will He save and keep.

His voice silences the waves,

With love that overcomes the graves.

I will not fear even death,

Until I take my dying breath.

Heal

In my pain, I fight for joy;
A blissful song will I employ.
In Him, I find my rest.
His plans for me are good and best.
Even as I wrestle and hurt,
He can bring beauty from the dirt.
The thief comes to destroy and steal,
But He comes to restore and heal.

Redeemed

You say I am redeemed,
More joy than I could have dreamed.
You heard my lament of distress,
And came to me in the muck and mess.
When I thought I was too far gone,
You assured me new hope would
dawn.
Many times, my life did you save;
In you, I have courage to be brave.

Cling

There is none greater,
I owe thanks to my Creator.
For me, He defeated death
And gave me life as I take a breath.
His love is full of might and power,
His Name is a strong tower.
No matter what this life will bring,
Onto His presence will I cling.

Conduit

You are a conduit of grace,
Your mercy fills the open space.
Your words are merciful and kind,
You soothe the troubled mind.
My burdens you gladly bear,
Your treasures you freely share.
Your own life you would give,
That I may thrive and live.

Scarlet

Though my sin was scarlet red,

For my redemption, He was dead.

But the grave failed to contain,

He arose to erase sin's stain.

From crimson, I am made clean like

snow.

Forever forgiven, His grace did show.

Indeed, He has set me free!

Death is defeated, mine is the victory.

Forever Kingdom

His blood poured out like a fountain.

Our faith in Him can move the

mountain.

He was silent even as His body broke,

Yet light and easy is His yoke.

He died so that we may thrive.

Death is defeated, we are alive!

All in Christ are granted freedom,

As we inherit His forever kingdom.

Light

Look to the radiance of the morning
star,
A glory that shines from afar.
Our hearts long and thirst for the light,
Though darkness tempts with all its
might.
He sits enthroned in all His splendor,
Yet loves with a heart so tender.
He sent His only Son to die,
That we may live and lift Him high.

Illuminates

Your light shines and illuminates;
Much power it demonstrates.
Though darkness tries to claw and bite,
It always surrenders to the light.
A flicker of hope can grow and swell,
To heal the sickness and make you
well.
Your strength is greater than you
know,
Even a little spark could grow.

Conquered

Pain was meant to be conquered,

Hopes will not be deferred.

Dreams can blossom and bloom,

No longer will sadness loom.

Darkness will cower and retreat,

As the enemy is crushed in defeat.

Anguish will finally cease,

As peace and blessing increase.

Dream

He appeared to me in a dream,
And shone bright with the sun's gleam.
He wore clothes of crystal white,
And beckoned me to come near the
light.
He told me my pain would be no more,
And be forgotten like the tales of yore.
He told me I would walk on streets of
gold,
And his hands forever I would hold.

Prophecy

I know of a love foretold,

Truth spun by prophets of old.

He would turn water into wine,

The last meal he would dine.

By his grace, the lame would walk

The dead would rise, the mute could

talk.

There is no brokenness he cannot cure,

Approach him with a faith childlike

and pure.

Sages

As your wisdom grows and ages,
You will dine with prophets and sages.
Your mercy is rooted deep,
As you comfort the mothers who weep.
Your insight is like a tree,
Old and rooted, yet tall and free.
Your faith is pure and young,
And your words sweeter than any song

ever sung.

Road

May you walk down the narrow road,
Even as you bear the heavy load.
Long and far are your journeys,
But in your light the darkness flees.
Every mountain that you climb,
You will triumph every time.
Take the street that leads back to me,
That we may go into infinity.

Cup

My cup, it runneth over.

My fortune is like a clover.

My pantry is full and my table

overflows,

I count my blessings despite how life

goes.

My bounty is teeming aplenty,

Abundant like the fish of the sea.

I have no reason to worry,

Only peace, no need for anxiety.

Loss

Though yours is a searing loss,
This Red Sea you will cross.
Though the enemy comes to maim,
A mighty victory you will claim.
As you look at the hurdles
insurmountable,
Did you know your strength is
incalculable?
You are a conqueror full of power,
You will stand firm like a strong tower.

Song

There is a melodious song,
Where lungs expand and breaths
prolong.
It is sweet harmony to the ears,
A sound that brings one to tears.
Every note in perfect placement,
There is only bliss, no disappointment.
This is the music that sets you free,
Sends you home in euphoric glee.

Pray

When you pray, your words ascend,
To the place where there is no end.
Hopes swell and arise,
And you gain your heavenly prize.
Lift up your eyes to the hills,
And see the steadfastness of windmills.
Your guilt and shame will be erased,
No matter the dark shadows you faced.

Ascend

To the heights of the mount I will
ascend,
The depth of your love there is no end.
When my soul takes flight,
I will migrate to the light.
I have walked through the fire,
But I will never retire.
I will endure in the name of love,
Find strength and glory from above.

Look at the Birds

Look at the birds of the sky,
Look at how freely they fly.
They float in the air with ease,
With no qualms on who to please.
They neither gather nor sow,
Yet always know where to go.
They soar with no trouble or worry,
Their flight is calm with no hurry.

Birdsongs

I am greeted by the birds' morning
song.

Sleep evades and the night is long.

The birds, they neither sow nor reap.

But the Father does bless and keep.

O, bird, why do you chirp with such
joy?

Your song, can I borrow and employ?

On your wings, I will fly and rise,

As my praises pierce heaven's skies.

Made in the USA
Monee, IL
06 July 2021